MW01109991

THE BUCKET LIST GUIDE TO ☑ FRIENDSHIP

BY STEPHANIE PETERS

CAPSTONE PRESS
a capstone imprint

Published by Capstone Press, an imprint of Capstone
1710 Roe Crest Drive, North Mankato, Minnesota 56003
capstonepub.com

Copyright © 2023 by Spark. All rights reserved. No
part of this publication may be reproduced in whole or
in part, or stored in a retrieval system, or transmitted
in any form or by any means, electronic, mechanical,
photocopying, recording, or otherwise, without written
permission of the publisher.

Library of Congress Cataloging-in-Publication Data is
available on the Library of Congress website.

ISBN: 9781669003755 (hardcover)
ISBN: 9781669003717 (ebook PDF)

Summary: What does it take to be a great friend?
Find out with the help of a bucket list. Learn how meet
new friends, maintain relationships with old ones, be
a good listener, and more in this easy-to-follow guide
guaranteed to help you tackle all the items on your
friendship bucket list.

Editor: Donald Lemke; Designer: Kay Fraser;
Media Researcher: Svetlana Zhurkin;
Production Specialist: Katy LaVigne

Image Credits
Getty Images: Alex Potemkin, 25, Cavan Images, 24,
fstop123, 4, kali9, 21, Robert Niedring, 11, xavierarnau,
cover (bottom left); Shutterstock: Antonio Guillem, 15,
Asier Romero, 23, BearFotos, 14, Daisy Daisy, 20, Diego
Cervo, 27, Elena Elisseeva, 26, Ground Picture, 10, 12,
Inside Creative House, 7, LightField Studios, 13, Max
Kegfire, cover (right), Monkey Business Images, cover
(bottom right), 16, 18, MPH Photos, 5, New Africa, 9,
P Maxwell Photography, 29, Prostock-studio, 8, Rido,
17, Tanya Terekhina, 28, VH-studio, 6, ViDI Studio, 22,
zentilia, 19

All internet sites appearing in back matter were
available and accurate when this book was sent to press.

CONTENTS

Words in **bold** appear in the glossary.

☑ BUDDY SYSTEM

What does it mean to be a good friend? How do you make new friends? Check out some useful tips and fun facts in this guide. Then check off your bucket list items as you create long-lasting friendships.

☑MEET AND GREET 101

Meeting people for the first time can be scary. Tackle that fear by focusing on friendly **gestures**. Learning how to put your best foot forward is a great bucket list item!

Making friends starts with a smile. Add a handshake, fist bump, or elbow tap—and *BOOM!* You're both closer to having a new friend.

DID YOU KNOW?

Ancient Greeks shook hands to show they came in peace. Their empty hands proved they didn't carry weapons.

WHAT'S IN A NAME?

Take time to learn someone's name. It tells that person that they matter to you. So add "remembering names" to your friendship bucket list! If you forget a name, just ask. That person has probably forgotten a name before too.

SAME! (AND NOT SAME!)

Good friends often like the same things. But it's OK if you don't! Opening yourself up to new experiences is a great bucket list item. Take time to find out the stuff your friend likes. You could end up liking those things too.

☑ BFFS OR A BUNCH OF BUDS?

Friendships work best when you know yourself first. Make it a bucket list item to understand what's important to you. Once you know that, opening up to others will be easier.

FRIEND COMFORT ZONE

Extroverts love being part of a large friend group. **Introverts** are happy having one or two best friends. Understanding your friend comfort zone can be a bucket list item.

QUALITY Q&A

Get to know someone better by asking questions about them. Listen carefully to the answers. Ask follow-up questions if you want to know more. Being a good listener is a key to strong friendships. Be sure it's on your bucket list!

JOIN THE CLUB

Want to grow your friend group? Clubs are a great place to meet people who share your interests. Start by checking out clubs at your school or in your city. Or add "Start My Own Club" to your bucket list! Then create a club for your favorite hobby or sport.

☑ THE COLORS OF FRIENDSHIP

What makes a good friend? When should you think about walking away from a friendship? Understanding the difference between good and bad friendships can help. It's an excellent goal for any bucket list.

Green means *go*! Green-light friends are honest and **supportive**. When you meet someone with these traits, you should *go* with that friendship!

Show your friend you trust them to steer you in the right direction!

19

RED FLAGS

Red flags are warning signs that something is not right. **Gossiping**, starting **rumors**, telling secrets, and making fun of others are all red flags. If someone shows these flags, you might need to decide if that person is really your friend.

No!

GRAY AREAS

Sometimes friends encourage you to try new activities. But what if a friend **pressures** you to do something you think is wrong? A true friend will understand if you say no. Still, saying no can be hard. Learning how can be a bucket list item.

IF THINGS GO WRONG

What do you do when a friendship is in trouble . . . or over? It might be difficult to let go. But it's important to accept when a friendship has run its course. Learning how to say goodbye to a friend should be on every friendship bucket list.

ARE WE CALLING IT QUITS?

Friendships end for many reasons. Maybe you moved away and lost touch. Maybe you're not interested in the same things anymore. Whatever the reason, it's hard to lose or let go of a friend.

Arguments between friends—even best friends—can happen. The first step to patching things up is talking about it. A good bucket list goal is learning to admit your mistakes, accept apologies, and then move forward.

WANT TO TRY MORE?

You've got all the important bucket list items for solid friendships! Now it's time to add some fun activities and experiences to your must-do list. Check out (and then check off) a few of these ideas. Then think of other items to add to the list. A bucket list is always changing and growing—just like you and your friendships!

☑ Share friendship bracelets.

☑ Make up a silly story together.

☑ Record a social media video.

☑ Go to a friend's special event.

☑ Make a silly sign to cheer on a friend.

☑ Go camping—inside or outdoors!

☑ Invite others into your friend group.

☑ Make a huge ice cream sundae and ENJOY!

GLOSSARY

extrovert (EK-struh-vurt)—an outgoing person who enjoys being with many other people

gesture (JESS-chur)— a movement usually of the body or limbs to express or emphasize an idea or attitude

gossip (GAH-sihp)—conversations or reports about other people involving details that are not confirmed as being true

introvert (IN-truh-vurt)—a shy person who prefers to spend time alone or with a few people

pressure (PRESH-ur)—strong influence or force

rumor (ROO-mur)— talk or opinion widely spread with no real source

supportive (suh-POHR-tiv)—providing encouragement or emotional help

READ MORE

Cooper, Scott. *Speak Up and Get Along!* Golden Valley, MN: Free Spirit Publishing, 2019.

Crohn, Joann. *Me and My Friendships: A Friendship Book for Kids*. Emeryville, CA: Rockridge Press, 2021.

Kennedy-Moore, Dr. Eileen and McLaughlin, Christine. *Growing Friendships: A Kids' Guide to Making and Keeping Friends.* New York: Aladdin, 2017.

INTERNET SITES

100+ Things for Teens to Do This Summer
studentden.com/100-things-for-teens-to-do-this-summer

How to Handle Peer Pressure
kidshealth.org/en/kids/peer-pressure.html#catfriend

Young Men's Health: Friendship Issues
youngmenshealthsite.org/guides/friendship

INDEX

ABOUT THE AUTHOR

Stephanie Peters has been writing books for young readers for more than 25 years. Among her most recent titles are *Sleeping Beauty: Magic Master* and *Johnny Slimeseed*, both for Capstone's Far-Out Fairy Tales and Folk Tales series. An avid reader, workout enthusiast, and beach wanderer, Stephanie enjoys spending time with her children, Jackson and Chloe, her husband, Dan, and the family's two cats and two rabbits. She lives and works in Mansfield, Massachusetts.